ESSAYS IN ENGLISH HISTORY

Books by Paul Harrison Silfen

Essays in English History

Essays in Russian History

*The Influence of the Mongols
on Russia: A Dimensional View*

*The Völkisch Ideology and the Roots of Nazism:
The Early Writings of Arthur Moeller van den Bruck*

Essays in
ENGLISH HISTORY

Paul Harrison Silfen

An Exposition-University Book

Exposition Press   Hicksville, New York

FIRST EDITION

© 1975 by Paul Harrison Silfen

Library of Congress Catalog Card Number: 74-80691

ISBN 0-682-48047-9

Printed in the United States of America

Contents

Contents

ESSAYS IN ENGLISH HISTORY

"Europe's history is the history of liberty."

WILLIAM H. MCNEILL,
The Shape of European History

God created humans and decided that they should always disagree. That is why He placed them in different dimensions . . . The fact that many couples live together happily is merely His way of glorifying Himself. As W. H. McNeill states: "In the fifth century, St. Augustine created an enduring distinctively Christian view of history which remained fundamental for Latin Christendom until the 17th century. Augustine emphasized Divine Providence and the mystery whereby each individual's free will, in ways that ran far beyond human ken, nevertheless remained subject to, and an instrument of, God's purposes for men."

I

English History
in Five Dimensions

God has continually given England great scientific men who have been able to achieve so much. Specifically there was Sir Isaac Newton (1642-1727). There will be many more great English scientists named in this book. I have all of Shakespeare's plays, and I do not believe that God erred when he made Shakespeare the greatest English playwright. I do not believe, for example, that when he made Shylock Jewish in *The Merchant of Venice* that he was wrong. God always knows best.

*English Rulers**

871-899	Alfred
1017-35	Canute
1042-66	Edward, the Confessor
1066	Harold II
1066-1087	William I (the Conqueror)
1087-1100	William II (William Rufus)
1100-35	Henry I
1135-54	Stephen

ANGEVINS AND PLANTAGENETS

1154-89	Henry II
1189-99	Richard I
1199-1216	John

*For the period prior to 1066, only major English rulers are listed.

ANGEVINS AND PLANTAGENETS

1216-72	Henry III
1272-1307	Edward I
1307-27	Edward II
1327-77	Edward III
1377-99	Richard II

LANCASTRIANS

1399-1413	Henry IV
1413-22	Henry V
1422-61 and 1470-71	Henry VI

YORKISTS

1461-83	Edward IV
1483	Edward V
1483-85	Richard III

TUDORS

1485-1509	Henry VII
1509-47	Henry VIII
1547-53	Edward VI
1553-58	Mary I
1558-1603	Elizabeth (the Great)

THE STUARTS

1603-25	James I
1625-49	Charles I
1649-60 Interregnum (Cromwell's dictatorship, etc.)	
1660-85	Charles II
1685-88	James II
1688-1702	William III and Mary II
1702-14	Anne

HANOVERIANS

1714-27	George I
1727-60	George II
1760-1820	George III
	(the king we revolted against)
	against)
1820-30	George IV
1830-37	William IV
1837-1902	Victoria
1901-10	Edward VII
1910-36	George V
1936	Edward VIII
1936-52	George VI
1952	Elizabeth II

ENGLAND—THE ROMAN PROVINCE[1]

Caesar visited England in 55-54 B.C. (which is Roman year 699) because the island tribes were linked with and helped by the Northern European tribes. The last Celtic invasions were made by the Belgic tribesmen in the first century B.C.

Pytheas of Marseilles circumnavigated the British Isles in the fourth century B.C. Herodotus in 445 B.C. had heard of the tin from the far western isles.

All Britains dyed their bodies blue with woad. Julius Caesar was forced to withdraw from England due to the attacks of Cassivellaunus, but undaunted, he proclaimed a Roman triumph after his second expedition was forced to withdraw in 54 B.C.

After Caligula's assassination in A.D. 41, the new Emperor Claudius gave orders for a new invasion of Britain in A.D. 43. A great revolt by Queen Boadicea in A.D. 60 was finally crushed by the Romans.

The Roman Agricula finished off the last British resistance at Mons Graupius in A.D. 78.

The villa system was the dominant feature of Romans in

England during the heyday of their control. It is thought that cities were always stagnant. The villas continued prosperous through the fourth century, and some even into the fifth. From A.D. 89 (in the time of Domitian) the Roman Empire was building continuous walls across Britain. The Emperor Hadrian came to England in A.D. 121 after the 10th Legion vanished completely in the north. This event is glorified in England, much as Custer's Last Stand is glorified in the United States by the Indian part of the population.

Emperor Severus arrived in A.D. 208 and brought stability to the island for one hundred years.

THE VIKINGS

The Vikings struck in England in A.D. 787. In the 790s they destroyed Northumbrian culture and in 842 they plundered London. By the 870s only Wessex remained unconquered by the Danes. It was saved by Alfred the Great in 878. During this period France was ravaged by the Normans. In 837, Antwerp was burned. In 841, Rouen suffered the same fate. In 845, Hamburg and Paris were the lucky cities. Even Charlemagne's old palace at Aachen was ravaged by the Vikings in 881. During the ninth century Europe was truly under siege.

Happily for that continent, King Arnulf crushed the Vikings on the Dyle River in 891. His victory decreased pressure on Germany. Unfortunately for the Germans, God then sent the Hungarians. The final result was that Rollo, a notorious Viking, was granted the Province of Normandy in France by the immortal king; Charles the Simple.

Vikings also invaded eastern Europe. Ireland was conquered by the Norwegians and the Danes in the 800s. Scandinavians settled Iceland between 875 and 930. The Vikings, known historically as great sailors, got to Greenland in the late 900s and even to North America about that time. There is a remnant of Norse culture to be found in the Irish sagas.

Swedish Vikings took Finland and sailed down European rivers deep into Russia to trade with Constantinople and Baghdad.

As a result the Byzantine Imperial guard was made up of Norsemen.

By the end of the ninth century, a Swedish expedition took Novgorod. In the tenth century, the Viking Rurik took Kiev and the Vikings established a strong state in that area. It is perfectly comprehensible that those Vikings, living among Russians, gradualy became somewhat Slavic. They were also influenced by Byzantium and God arranged that the official religion of Russia should be the Eastern Orthodox branch of Christianity.

The development of strong monarchs in Scandinavia tamed the Vikings by the middle of the eleventh century. Late in that century Scandinavian raiders became soldiers for the East Roman Empire. The threat from Scandinavia was over as they had all been converted to Eastern Orthodox Christianity. However, it must be noted charitably that the Vikings were not entirely barbarians. They excelled at commerce as well as piracy, and they were the greatest seafarers of the age. They introduced Europe to the art of ocean navigation and immeasurably enlarged the horizons of the West. In a word, they injected a spirit of enterprise and cosmopolitanism into the parochial conservatism of the Carolingian rulers.

It might be mentioned that it was the misfortune of the Chinese that they never had any good healthy Scandinavian raids to inspire them to become seafarers. Had that happened, God alone knows whether the Indians would have been speaking Chinese when Columbus got here.

FEUDALISM

A turning point in the history of Western Christendom was witnessed during the latter half of the eleventh century. The Normans played a dominant part in the transformations which then occurred.[2]

At 1050 the fundamental character remains the great universal decline in population.

Advances after 1050 not only led to English relations with the East becoming easier and more intimate, but most important is the fact that they changed their character.

Formerly such relations had been almost exclusively as an importer. Following 1050 the West became a great supplier of manufactured goods.

The Second Feudal Age was characterized both by men's need to group themselves in larger communities and by a clearer general consciousness of themselves. *Patriotism* became the outward manifestation of these latent qualities and so in its turn the creator of new realities.

When, in 1170, Henry II with a single stroke removed from office all the sheriffs in the kingdom, he subjected their administrations to an inquest and reappointed only a few of them. Thereupon it was plain to everyone that throughout England the king was master of those who governed in his name. Because the public office of sherriff could not completely be identified with the fief, England was henceforth a truly unified state. It was the historian Marc Block's wisdom to state this had occurred much earlier than any other continental kingdom. It was England's misfortune not to realize that American revolutionaries of 1776 took the title of Continental Congress seriously. God decided that America would win the entire continent.

ENGLAND BETWEEN 1066 AND 1466

After William's victory at Hastings in A.D. 1066, the state was entirely his property. This helps to explain the different courses of political evolution to the north and south of the Channel, though the historian Wallace K. Ferguson gives additional reasons.

From the reign of Louis VII (1137-80) to that of Philip Augustus (1180-1223) the royal power made progress that cannot be explained merely by the genius of the king. (Perhaps God wished it.) It was due very largely to the economic and social transformation occasioned by the *development of the bourgeoise.*

The Battle of Bouvines in 1215 was the first of the great European battles and, if we except Waterloo, no other battle had such vast, immediate consequences. In Germany, Otto IV of Brunswick (1198-1215) was replaced by Frederick II.

In England, John Lackland, who had been humiliated by Bouvines, saw the barons rise against him and force his acceptance of the great charter (Magna Carta).

In France territorial conquests were assured by the Treaty of Chinon; feudality was vanquished in the person of Ferrand of Portugal; and the royal power, which had just proved its strength by defeating the external enemy, was, in the eyes of the people, invested with a national prestige that endowed it with twofold vigor.

Frederick Barbarossa, King of Germany (1152-90), realized that to insure a territorial base outside the country, he would have to act. Hence the marriage of his son Henry to Constance, heiress of the kingdom of Sicily, was arranged in 1184. In order to survive, the House of Hohenstaufen was obliged to denationalize itself, turning from Germany to Italy.

This shows the importance of the later papal defeat of the Holy Roman Empire that had been centered in Germany. The cause of the papacy was the cause of the Church. As such it was bound up with the liberty of the European states to such an extent that the victory of Philip Augustus at Bouvines was the triumph of both causes.

A strongly worded disagreement with opinion is to be found in Geoffrey Barraclough's books. He believes that the triumph of the papacy ruined Germany. Wallace K. Ferguson agrees with him totally.

Just like Ecclesiastical law, theology was essentially an achievement of the thirteenth century. The scholastic philosophy, as God had given it during all the previous centuries, found its climax in the *Summa Theologica* of Thomas Aquinas, 1274.

During Edward II's reign (1307-27) Parliament developed greatly. The Great Council turned into today's House of Lords and the peerage of England originated during his reign. In addition, the joint meetings of the knights of the shires with the burghers in the towns eventually turned into the House of Commons, and the process of impeachment was instituted.

The system of justices of the peace began under Edward III

(1327-77), but it was not until much later, during the reign
of Henry VI (1422-61) that all knights of the shire got to vote
for the first time. Thus, we can see that God's working out of
the English system of government was a long and painful process
which is still continuing.

THE TUDOR PERIOD

In discussing the reign of Richard III (1483-85), a previous
king of England, Henry VI, is seen by Lacey Baldwin Smith as
"saintly," which just proves that God can send down saints of
many kinds.[3] In 1485, the Wars of the Roses were brought to a
violent end at the battle of Bosworth. Henry VII (1484-1509)
was victorious because most of the key nobles deserted Richard
III, and a king of England without soldiers was a dead man.

Smith says that the Tudor Period was contradictory.[4] I
would strongly prefer using the word dimensional. I think that
word is eternal just as all editions of the Bible are eternal. Every
version of the Bible, for instance, discusses the Exodus.

God's work in history is seen very clearly when one knows
just where to look. For example, England in 1485 was very much
like Russia during its Time of Troubles[5] which ended in 1538
and began the Romanoff Dynasty which continued until 1917.
God is not to be trifled with because all of the sicknesses that
He has mentioned in the Torah are not included in His arsenal
of illness. Specifically, the Black Death, which struck England
between 1348 and 1350, was not mentioned in the Torah.

It is remarkable to me that the English colonized most of
Africa. England was such a tiny country, having in 1700 a population of about six milion people. However, it seems undeniable
that the English are among God's chosen peoples.

England's closeness to God is strongly brought home to me by
the fact that between 1500 and 1800 unprecendented prosperity
existed on that little island. I feel very strongly that the inflation
from which America is suffering in 1974 is coming directly from
God just as the English inflation did.[6]

Smith discusses the various threats to the Tudor throne in

1485, and God alone knows how many there were.[7] The chief threat to the throne of Henry VII (1485-1509) came from Elizabeth of York, and the king solved that Lancastrian threat by marrying the girl. I recently had a good thought when I realized that American astronauts in 1973 are very much like the first colonists who came to the New World after Columbus discovered it in 1492.

Two pretenders to the throne of Henry VII were Lambert Simnel and Perkin Warbuck. Simnel was defeated at the Battle of Stoke in 1487 and Warbeck was hanged in 1499.

Henry VII had five children, and one of them, Margaret, was sent to Scotland where she married James IV, of Scotland which may explain why Elizabeth the Great chose a Scottish cousin for her successor. Thus the Stuart dynasty got into England.

In the sixteenth century practically all the land in England was held by some feudal title.[8] In 1492 Henry VII was rewarded by the king of France for giving up his claim to the throne of France.[9]

God was long preparing England for its place in the sun during these years, for throughout the reign of Henry VII a revolution in finances was going on,[10] which was much like Russia during the Time of Troubles. England lost many of its leading noblemen during its Wars of the Roses. That is why the first parliament of Henry VII had only eighteen barons. One of the most infamous institutions in English history, the Court of the Star Chamber, was used by Henry VII.[11]

In 1510, English businessmen wrested control of St. Paul's school from the English churchman, Dean Colet, which shows that, unlike most of the rest of the world, English churchmen were being integrated into a growing capitalist society.[12]

Smith states that in the England of those days "God's grace was considered to be above justice."[13] He points out that England never lost its religious feeling for the Lollards and the ideas of John Wycliffe (1320?-84) which finally led to the Anglican Church.

Another parallel betwwen English and Russian history is seen in the fact that in 1536 England experienced the Pilgrimage of Grace, which is dimensionally parallel to Stenka Razin's revolt against the nobility in Russia in 1640.

A revolt in Scotland was smashed in 1547 by the Duke of Somerset (1506-52) who was then the Protector of the English Parliament. That English history has all the necessary dimensional requirements is obvious to me from the fact that the great churchman John Knox (1505?-72) was thundering against the "regiment of women" because he did not believe there should be so many female ruling monarchs. He was an early exponent of male chauvinism.

The dimensional relations between England and France are brought out quite clearly where it is shown that after the accidental death of France's King Henry II (1519-59), Elizabeth I (1558-1603) dominated Europe. During her reign the Jesuits seemed to be a constant danger to England. Under Pope Paul IV (1555-59) the Jesuits were looked on as fellow travelers. (Similarly many innocent people were hurt during the McCarthy era of the United States.) Queen Elizabeth I is known for use of her virginity as a diplomatic weapon. Elizabeth II passed up the chance to do the same.

All English people are familiar with the great reign of Queen Elizabeth I (1558-1603).[14] Fewer are familiar with the French queen, Mary of Guise.[15] That period saw much violence going on in England just as the elegant reign of Elizabeth did. In Freudian terms, it is easy to understand how the value of Elizabeth I's maidenhead aided her diplomatically.

Smith describes King James I (1603-25) as not having been overly clean.[16] It is also stated that he refused to show himself to his subjects because he felt that he was being asked to pull down his pants and show "his ars!"[17] Nonetheless, as James VI, he was a good king in Scotland.[18] His chief error was that he mistook London for Edinburgh.[19] Ironically, he wrote a book called, *The Trew Law of Free Monarchies*[20] just as Hitler wrote *Mein Kamp*.

James, being a typical Scottish king, was totally unaware of the need for economy in governing England. That ignorance on his part caused him to use his royal funds to reward his friends. As Smith points out, by 1625, the end of James's reign, the English crown was near to collapse by the king's weakness of character. English women at the court "tore him to pieces with their tongues."[21]

By 1603, James had inherited a severe financial crisis.[22] In part, James's financial problems related dimensionally back to the reign of Elizabeth the Great because the cost of the wars she waged with Spain and Ireland against France had become part of the national debt. Because of James's troubles, the English Parliament formed the Committee of the Whole, which in 1607 stripped the Speaker in the House of Commons of all control over parliamentary debates.[22]

There are in the history of England far more dimensional elements than any American can possibly conceive of. Today we are greatly concerned about Watergate, an incident in which some criminals broke into Democratic headquarters and were caught. In England, under James I, there was the scandal involving Robert Carr, who became the King's Favorite after breaking a leg at a joust held while James was present. Carr, in 1613, decided to marry Lady Francis Howard. One of the king's friends, Thomas Overbury, was strongly against the match. Carr had Overbury thrown into prison and poisoned and the Carr-Howard marriage followed directly.[23]

The history of England has in it countless figures who, because of their friendship with various kings, were able to divert the course of the country. For example, the Duke of Buckingham at one point had an income of £80,000 which came from the royal treasury at a time when the debt of England stood at £90,000.[24]

Throughout the history of England, God caused religious disputes which violently affected the history of the country. The Puritans had placed high hopes in James and looked to him to be their Moses.[25]

In 1604, at the Hampton Court Conference, James showed himself to be strikingly similar to Adolph Hitler. At that conference he made it perfectly clear that he wanted only one belief in the English Church. All sectarianism was forbidden.

One figure who enabled James I to rule England as well as he did was Robert Cecil, the Earl of Salisbury. Cecil preferred to remain in the background like a gray eminence who manipulated people for the benefit of his country. In 1604, he enabled England to get a treaty of peace with Spain.

Very important historically was the 1606 Bate's Case which decided that the king could arbitrarily increase customs duties in England.[26] This became one of the causes for the fighting called the English Civil War. But as Smith shows, it was the selling of crown lands that ruined the Stuart monarchs, though devoted Englishmen like Robert and William Cecil attempted again and again to reconcile those kings from Scotland with the English system of government. In 1610, the Great Contract, which Robert Cecil had striven to arrange, failed in Parliament. To get even with him, James I gradually dispensed with his services.[27]

Obviously, the English people were getting angrier and angrier with the Stuart king. The Second Parliament of 1614 was dissolved because it refused to grant the king any money.[28] In order to get funds from somewhere, James invented the title of baronet and sold it to wealthy Englishmen.[29]

James's intimate friend, the Duke of Buckingham, who, around 1618 made ludicrous attempts to ease diplomatically God's religious wars that were raging throughout Europe, was also one of the prime causes for the downfall of the Stuarts.

A little-noted figure historically, Ferdinand of Styria, was the Catholic and pro-Hapsburg, emperor of the Holy Roman Empire, and his actions were decisive in upsetting the religious balance in Europe.[30]

The elements of the whole affair are humorous. There was the Duke of Buckingham's going off with a "close" friend, the future king of England, Charles I, both of them in disguise. They wore false beards on a journey to Spain, where Charles attempted to woo the Spanish princess in English fashion. The shocked lady was speechless but finally rebuffed him pointedly.[31]

It is undeniable that King Charles I had been programmed by

God to dream.[32] Karl Marx, the father of communism, proved that monetary factors were crucial throughout. Two taxes which Parliament cut—tonnage and poundage—reduced the royal income and angered the Stuart monarch. (But God is very impartial and He kept providing different means of illegally raising money.) In 1640, Charles I employed the Court of Wards solely as a means of raising money.[33] Another unconstitutional means which Charles tried was the imposition of ship money in 1634.[34] Legally, English towns on the coast could be required to pay ship money to the king for their defense against invasion. Charles I's sin was demanding that money be paid by inland towns in no conceivable danger.

There is a strange parallel between the reign of Charles I in England and that of Catherine the Great (1762-96) in Russia. Dimensionally speaking, a great popular source of England's annoyance was the king's French queen. The Long Parliament elected in 1640 refused to permit the king to dissolve it without its own consent. This opposition to the kings by constitutional means led to the English Civil War and the beheading of Charles I.

A great figure in that opposition to the King, was John Pym.[35] (One book written about him is entitled *King Pym.*) It is interesting that in the eyes of the king, Pym's cardinal sin was his desire to impeach the king's French wife. (It will be recalled that sex is one of my new dimensions.) Henrietta Maria, Catholic Frenchwoman, firmly believed in her right to rule England.*

One of the most important parliamentary steps taken against Charles I was the Militia Bill, passed by Parliament in February 1642. It took from the king all control over the finances of the army.[36]

The English Civil War began on August 22, 1642, when Charles I raised his standard at Nottingham and, dimensionally speaking, we all know who came out on top in that.

During the Civil War, Englishmen on the parliamentary side strove to be as unrevolutionary as possible.[37] Nonetheless, the

---

*Like the wife of the last Russian czar, Nicholas II (1815-1917), Czarina Alexandra.

war did involve bloody battles and, as Hitler never learned, the
English, when they fight, do so in a very permanent, deadly
fashion.

One of the great battles of the Civil War took place in
Marston Moor in July 1644. The royalists were defeated at
Naseby in 1645 by the New Model Army, led by Sir Thomas
Fairfax. His assistant was Oliver Cromwell.

In the Smith book Cromwell is quoted as saying when he
raised the English army, "Haste . . . The enemy in all probability
will be in our bowels in ten days."[38]

II

England in the Nineteenth and Twentieth Centuries

THE IRISH QUESTION

Ireland was Europe's worst minority problem after 1801. Ireland had been incorporated with England and was just one part of Great Britain as a defensive measure against Napoleon. Even at that time the Irish objected, which explains why Irish members of Parliament were obstructionists in those years.

The peasants, helpless against absentee landlords, most of whom lived in London, were worse off in the nineteenth century than French peasants had been in 1789!

The collecting of tithes by the Catholic Church in Ireland led to the establishment of Anglicanism, which was not much more popular than the previous religion but was much more permanent, since the Anglican Church owned much of the land in Ireland.

William Gladstone, during his first ministry (1868-74), disestablished the Church of Ireland and initiated measures to protect Irish farm tenants. By 1900, under three Conservative governments, Irish tenants were being urged by the English government to buy out their landlords.

Ireland tried for Home Rule in 1886. Gladstone split his Liberal Party in this attempt, and Liberal-Unionists opposed their own leader. The Conservatives rallied around Joseph Chamberlain.[1]

After a Home Rule Bill had finally been passed in 1914, agitation in Ulster led to the establishment of the Irish Free State. The leader of the Irish in these years was Randolph Churchill, whose slogan was "Ulster will fight, and Ulster will be right."

Ulster took that slogan to heart and has been fighting ever since.[2]

For the most part, Ulster was populated by Presbyterians from the north of Ireland. To the best of this author's knowledge, there is no good book on the Liberal-Unionists.

The Ulster men were backed by British Conservative Standard Army, drilled to resist the 1914 Act of Parliament which authorized Home Rule, and Great Britain. Only the outbreak of World War I prevented a civil war in England, then suffering from something of the nationalistic spirit that afflicted Austria-Hungary.[3]

During World War I, Home Rule was suspended, and after considerable violence on both sides, Catholic Ireland (Eire) in 1922 received dominion status. But eventually, in the 1930s, it dissolved all ties with Britain. (In 1890, Charles Stewart Parnell and Captain O'Shea were involved in a famous scandal.)[4]

There were two partitions of Ireland, with Ulster remaining part of the United Kingdom.

ENGLAND IN 1815

At Waterloo, England was halfway through the Industrial Revolution. A boom in iron, coal, and engineering reached its height around 1830 when the building of railroads began. In 1815, England was mainly a land of small towns. The enclosure process was completed and agriculture was efficient.

A new wealthy class had arisen and they paid increased attention to social evils. Ironically, the increased attention was exemplified by an unbelievably ferocious crime code which was perhaps the main feature in regard to social affairs after 1815.

From 1811 to 1820 England was under the regency of George IV, the son of George III, who is immortal because of his leadership of the British during the American Revolution. In 1815, the prime minister was Lord Liverpool. Parliament was increasing in strength while the institution of monarchy was losing strength. England was still dominated by the country gentry either as squires or as justices of the peace.

Under George III the House of Lords had switched from a

Whig to a Tory majority, a change accomplished mainly by the appointment of Sir William Pitt. At that time there were more peers in the cabinet than in the House of Commons. This was a most important development in the government of England, *i.e.,* the increased granting of peerages used by the king to pack the House of Lords.

In England at that time the political party lines were still unclear (*i.e.,* Tories or Conservatives were any persons who were against the Jacobins). Some of the Whigs were in favor of gradual reform. The Radicals, since they were open to new approaches and new methods, held the future in their hands. Edmund Burke's book, *Reflections on the Revolution in France,* published in 1790, became the bible of the Conservatives. He opposed all reform.

Internationally, England's power rested on her superior industrial and commercial techniques. The general degree of national unity was also a crucial factor. Most important was the English navy which dominated the seas.

One of the important political movements at that time was *Benthamism.* Jeremy Bentham's emphasis on "the greatest good for the greatest number" led to the philosophy of social reform advocated by James and John Stuart Mill.

ENGLAND AFTER 1815—FORCES OF CHANGE

The Corn Laws of 1815 and 1828 led to the first split between the landed and the manufacturing interests, coinciding with the outbreak of conflict between owners and workers. The years 1830 to 1850 constituted the era of rivers and steamships. Robert Owen was the father of English socialism. Lord Shaftesbury, the father of all nineteenth-century factory legislation, pushed the governing classes into assuming some responsibility for the welfare of the people. The Factory Act of 1833 was his achievement. John Stuart Mill restated utilitarianism as *democratic radicalism.*

After 1815, the mood of the lower classes aimed for domestic reform. Francis Place and William Lovett were important figures

in this period. It was during this period that the Combination
Acts were repealed, 1824.

John Himes, an important figure in Parliament, helped to
advocate that repeal. However, many strikes occurred immediately
after the Factory Act was repealed, so a new act was passed in
1825 which limited, but did not prevent, the rise of trade unions.
The great union created by Robert Owen, called the Grand
National Consolidated Trades Union, was too ambitious and
collapsed in 1834. Its collapse coincided with the shooting by
government troops of certain workers at Tolpuddle. The dead
were immortalized as the Tolpuddle martyrs.

The pressure of the Corn Law League on the government
had been like that placed on modern political parties. A further
push for English reformers resulted from the great Irish Famine.
The Corn Laws were repealed in 1846 by Robert Peel's Tory
government. This change in 1846 showed that the industrialists,
committed to an international economy, had become the governing
element in England.

Events in the world at that time also depended on English
control of the sea (which God has now given to the United
States). English control of the sea was continued by Lord
Palmerston. A British subject, Don Pacifico, was defended in
Greece by Palmerston's sending the British fleet. The Chinese
ship *Arrow,* however, flying the British flag, was attacked, giving
Palmerston his excuse to use the British navy to blast Chinese
cities such as Canton. The Second Anglo-Chinese War followed
and English armaments again proved superior to Chinese fire-
crackers.

According to Palmer the years 1830-32 began the period
of domination by the propertied classes of Europe who had a
large stake in English social development. It was they who pro-
vided the key liberal doctrine.[5]

Landed Tories protected labor in England but not in France.
After 1830 came the Golden Age of the Bourgeoisie—"golden"
because they had no problems with the lower class.

The French Minister Guizot and the English writer Macaulay

felt that democracy would bring disaster. Economically Western Europe continued to accumulate capital and to establish excellent corporations. The factory system spread from Western Europe. In England iron output increased 300 percent from 1830 to 1848. It increased only 65 percent in France, which is still a backward country despite its colorful past.

The building of railroads began in earnest after 1840. In the same year the Cunard trans-Atlantic service boats began crossing the oceans. England exported much capital.

In 1839, Europe owned $200 million worth of United States stock.

In England the labor movement had long been estranged from the government and the same was true in France. English democrats in particular felt cheated. The English workingmen struggled for economic and social reform. Economists invented the concept of the "labor market."

The New Poor Law of 1834 was especially hated by English workingmen because it made so unpleasant any attempt by them to obtain governmental relief. When workingmen were forced to enter the workhouses it was particularly shameful. A man forced to enter a workhouse was separated from his wife because regulations required the sexes to be segregated.

Labor unions were formed to improve the conditions of the working classes. Some repudiated the entire capitalistic system, urging a system where goods were produced for use, not for sale, and in which the workingmen would be compensated according to their need and not according to the requirements of their employer. Thus was the basis for most forms of socialism expounded in England during that earlier day.

Socialism spread rapidly in England after 1830 as it did in France where it was connected to revolutionary republicanism.

In England socialistic ideas were traditionally connected to Parliamentary reform. In 1838, a mass movement developed, the leaders of which were anti-capitalistic. This movement, known as Chartism, emphasized getting workingmen into Parliament. In 1839 that organization held a convention in London. "Char-

tism" has now become a dangerous word. In that year, and again
in 1842, petitions were sent to the House of Commons. The 1842
petition had three million signatures. Statistics claim that it was
signed by half the males in England. It was naturally rejected
by the House of Commons whose leaders asserted that political
democracy threatened property rights.

The movement gradually died down, but it was revived briefly
in 1848. By then, however, the English working classes had
shifted their emphasis away from getting a public charter granting
their rights and were putting most of their strength into forming
labor unions.

Between 1815 and 1848 Europe had achieved stabilization.
Then, as now, there existed in Europe two camps—the western
one to which England belonged and the eastern one to which
Russia belonged. The western camp favored nationalism; the
eastern camp opposed it. The western camp became increasingly
rich, liberal, and bourgeoise. However, the socialists' problem
was still unsolved in the west because all work was still being done
by that group known scornfully in England as the "working
class."

"Everywhere there was repression—in varying degrees, and
everywhere apprehension, more in some places than in others;
but there was also hope, confidence in the progress of the industrial and scientific society, and faith in the unfinished program of
the rights of man."[6]

The result of that hope was the great year of European
revolution—1848.

CLOSING YEARS OF THE NINETEENTH CENTURY

Gladstone, who became prime minister in 1868, was, according to the historian Massingham,[7] a great speaker. He elevated
the tone of the entire House of Commons and historians have
noted that his conversations with Queen Victoria sounded as if
he were addressing a public meeting.

The Conservative Party, not to be outdone, added liberal
legislation. Not sensitive to pressure from business interests, they

favored a laissez-faire economic policy, in this way continuing the tradition of the real Tory reformers.

They also took the initiative in labor legislation. They strengthened existing acts regulating conditions in the mines and factories. The laws regulating conditions in the factories were codified under Disraeli's second ministry (1874-80).

It was no secret to the upper classes that Disraeli was of Jewish descent, but despite intense British prejudices, he was able to rise to the highest elected post in the British government. As prime minister, he pushed through laws for social welfare and sanitation. His firm belief in imperialism was obvious as he arranged British control of the Suez Canal in 1875.

Around the turn of the century the Labor Party organization was transformed with many persons insisting on protective measures to counteract poor health, low income, and economic insecurity of the British working people.

The Liberals had abandoned the lower classes.[8] The British government's traditional laissez-faire policy was now altered and the Labor Party sponsored government intervention and social legislation on behalf of the workingman.

The dominant political parties during this age were the Liberals and the Tories. The rise of democracy in England was far more gradual than the same process in France. It was also probably more permanent.

Reform bills were passed in 1832 and 1867. The 1832 bill permitted one-eighth of the adult males to vote. The bill passed in 1867 was a result of Disraeli allied with the Whigs. That resulted in one-third of the adult males acquiring the vote. England has not yet recovered.

In 1884, the Liberal Party passed another act which gave three-quarters of the males in England the vote. Agricultural laborers, servants living with their employers, and unmarried grown sons living with their parents were excluded. (To celebrate England's victory in World War I, the year 1918 saw universal manhood suffrage achieved in England. Women's liberation was also strong that year because women over thirty were allowed to vote accompanied by a parent.)

Gradually, the ruling classes were being broadened, which was understandable because "good sportsmanship" always prevailed. The Labor Party had pioneered in new legislation during William Gladstone's first ministry (1868-74) and much had been achieved:

1. The principle of state-supported private education for all classes was established.
2. Secret ballots were introduced.
3. Labor unions were legalized definitely.
4. The purchase and sale of general commissions in the military was eliminated.
5. Oxford and Cambridge abolished religious entrance examinations, enabling all English to graduate.

TWENTIETH-CENTURY ENGLAND

The first ministry of the Liberal Asquith was 1908-16. During that period Lloyd George put through a spectacular program of social legislation—sickness, accident, old age, and a degree of unemployment insurance. These laws, once adopted, gave the English a sense of social well-being from the cradle to the grave. A modern minimum-wage law was also enacted. Liberal exchanges were established and restrictions on strikes and labor organizations were removed, partly as a follow-up to the famous 1901-02 Taff-Vale Case, in which a union was held liable for the acts of its individual members.

The second Lloyd George budget, passed in 1909, called for a progressive income and inheritance tax. "In effect advancing the novel idea of using taxation to modify the extremes of wealth and poverty."[9] Lloyd George called his 1909 budget a "war budget" for the war on poverty. It was directly aimed at the landed aristocracy and the power of the House of Lords was cut even further in the Act of 1911 which limited the veto power of the House of Lords in money matters and permitted them only a two-year delay on other things.

Government salaries to members of Parliament were increased

in order to overcome the Osborne Judgment of 1911. Between 1911 and 1912 there was a great deal of labor unrest. In these years there were great coal and railroad strikes. "Real wages" showed a tendency to fall after 1900.[10]

ENGLISH EDWARDIAN LIBERALISM TO 1910

There had been extreme unrest in England in 1905. The parliamentarian Campbell-Bannerman had become the leader of the Liberal Party in 1898 and by 1905, when he became prime minister, he was extremely popular. He had led the Liberal Party constantly to the left.

Very quietly during this period, Winston Churchill rose in the Colonial Office.[11] Also during this period labor representatives were first elected in strength—fifty-three of them in 1905. Joseph Chamberlain died at this time at the age of seventy-eight. Campbell-Bannerman remained prime minister until April, 1908. His greatest triumph had been the settlement of the war in South Africa where he gave the Transvaal complete self-government. The House of Commons passed the Trades Disputes Bill, but other pro-labor bills were killed by the House of Lords. The attacks began to give decisive power to the House of Commons.

Lloyd George moved forward with non-party bills and he established a single port of London authority. English minister Haldane was also important. He reformed the British army to make it similar to the German army and created the General Staff.

Women suffragettes began evidencing militancy in 1905 and this was critically viewed as setting the first example of rule breaking that endangered democracy. Advocates of women's liberation would never have made it to first base in England.

During these years there was a dangerous international situation. Lord Grey authorized military connections with France after conversations with Asquith, Campbell-Bannerman, and Haldane; however, the whole Cabinet was not a party to his negotiations.

The treaty with Russia about Persia, which Lord Grey spon-

sored, passed the House of Commons in 1907 and, according
to some historians, it drove the Russians back to the Balkans.
It might be mentioned that consciously the Russians had never
left the Balkans.

The year 1907 saw the substitution of the term "dominions"
for colonies. Campbell-Bannerman fell as prime minister in 1908
and Asquith with Lloyd George and Winston Churchill became
the dominant figures in the English government. The 1908 budget made the first annual allowance for old-age pensions. There
was a rejection of the liquor licensing bill by the House of Lords,
and historians feel that this showed that the House of Lords was
disrupting the constitution.

Internationally, Russia and Austria-Hungary united to im-
pede the reforms of the young Turks. Austria annexed Bosnia
and Herzogovinia. Serbia was humiliated when Germany sup-
ported Austria-Hungary in such a way that England concluded
the Germans were aiming for war.

At this time a *Daily Telegraph* interview with Kaiser
Wilhelm II showed him as an Anglophile ruler, but showed simultaneously that Germany was an enemy of England. The German
naval threat led to the building of eight dreadnaughts in 1909.
Lloyd George's budget of that year, upset by this, was vetoed by
the House of Lords. This led to the calling of a general election in
1909 on the constitutional issue of the right of the House of
Lords to veto a budget passed by the House of Commons. The
Liberal Party won a great victory. Its majority, however, depended
on Irish and labor votes. This group united at last on the
issue of limiting the House of Lords and giving Ireland Home
Rule. There was sorrow in England when King Edward died in
May, 1910.

III

Colonialism and Imperialism

Imperialism began as a crusade—a push of all white-man civilizations. It would bring enlightenment to those who still sat in darkness. The general feeling in each country was that it had its "mission." The British had the "white man's burden"; the French had their "mission civilicatrice"; and the Germans had the task of diffusing *Kultur*.

Both social Darwinism and popular anthropology taught that the white races were "fitter" or more gifted than the colored races. Kipling in 1899 wrote "Take up the White Man's burden, send out the best you breed, go bind your sons to exile, to serve your captive needs; to wait in heavy harness, on fettered folk and wild, your new-caught, sullen peoples, half devil and half child." That poem was written as criticism of the United States actions in both the Philippines and Cuba.

THE DUTCH, THE BRITISH, AND
THE RUSSIANS IN ASIA

Dutch colonies in the East Indies, especially India and Indonesia were ideal colonies for the "new imperialism." Year after year these colonies had surplus exports, thus they were perfect for the Dutch. A surplus of exports was the hallmark of a developed colonial area geared closely to the world market, with low purchasing power for the natives. It was kept going by foreign investment and management. These colonies had natural, rich, and varied tropical resources, and therefore did not compete with Western Europe. They also had much internal business which aided the mother country. Both where divided by religion and language and were therefore easy to rule. They had been conquered. Both were ruled by an honest civil service, *i.e.,* upper classes in both countries valued their empire as fields of opportunity for their sons. Both were benevolent despotisms. By curbing warfare, plague, and famine, both allowed the populations of their new respective areas to increase.

Java (Dutch East Indies) had 5 milion people in 1815. The population had risen to 48 milion by 1942. The population of India increased from 200 million to 400 million in 1942. Both India and Java were ideal for colonization because no foreign power directly challenged either the Dutch or the English. The Dutch position in Java was preserved by mutual jealousy between the English and the Germans. The English were, of course, in Singapore. The Dutch were in both the Malay Peninsula and Borneo. The French, entering the imperialistic competition, took over Indochina in the 1860s. They offered to give up Saigon in 1950.[1] In the 1880s, the Germans gained colonies in East Guinea, and in the Marshall and Solomon Islands.

The Dutch took over Java and their other holdings in order to prevent other European nations from colonizing these areas. They acted to put down native pirates and to find raw materials that they claimed the world demanded. They spread over the whole three-hundred-mile archipelago, substituting their empire for an old chain of Dutch trading posts and ruling angry Indonesians by something called, in their translation, "a culture system," in which the authorities required farmers to deliver as a kind of tax amounts of stated crops. They also favored teaching prospective colonists the Malay language.

The Dutch were resisted most strongly by the Mohammedan people in Java, and in 1830, 1849 and 1888 angry Indonesians revolted against them. Panislamism was very popular around 1914.

The English in India very openly regarded native beliefs as respulsive. They outlawed "Suttee," the Indian practice of burning a widow on the funeral pyre of her husband. They also suppressed the groups of religious murderers known as "Thugs." All this contributed to the 1957 Indian Mutiny, the revolt of the Sepays—Indians who had been trained by the British military to fight for the British government. The revolt led the

British to conclude that they must rule India with and through the Indians themselves and resulted in collaboration between the imperial powers and India's upper classes.

Native industry and native crafts collapsed before modern industrialism, reinforced by political power. Free trade was made possible by military superiority—an unusual fact generally overlooked by economists, though it turned Britain into the world's workshop and India into a supplier of raw jute, tea, oil, seeds, Indigo, and wheat.

In England business boomed, and India came to have the densest railroad network outside Europe and North America. As an interesting sidelight it might be mentioned that during this same period the English government was allowing many privileges to the French in Quebec.[2]

One of the great figures in the history of England was Thomas Macaulay, whose influence had made the English government, even before the mutiny, instruct their Indian subjects in English. After the mutiny, some Indians were let into the Governor's Council and some were allowed to develop, in India, land owned by Indians. As a result Indian businessmen began to demand more control of their country.

The predominately Indian National Congress was organized in 1885. In 1906 the All-India Muslim League was organized. The English, during this period being God's chosen people, exploited the different sects in India.

Nationalism spread in India throughout World War I as progress in self-rule was never fast enough. A conflict over India developed between the English and Russian governments. The Russians had been in Northern Asia since the seventeenth century disguised as Asiatics. They resumed pressure on inner Asia in 1850. But the markets, the demand for raw materials, and the demand for the investment of capital did not count for much. The explanation here is simply and purely Freudian.

Russia had a sense of mission, but Russian expansion was distinctively political in that most of the initiative came from the government. The czars sought a warm-water port and in 1860 Russia got Vladivostok on the Sea of Japan, but the main push by Russian imperialists was in Western Asia. In 1864, Russia took Tashkent which made the English fear for their Indian empire.

Afghanistan was a scene of conflict between England and Russia until 1875. In that year an Anglo-Russian agreement gave a large tongue of land to Afghanistan and so separated Russia and the Indian empire.

RUSSIAN PRESSURE ON PERSIA

Tiflis and Baku had been Persian. The whole country was now threatened; however English influence was strong on the seacoast in 1864, and an English company built the first Persian telegraph line. In 1890, the English government granted a large loan to Persian Gulf shiekdoms, taking the customs receipts of these small states as collateral. In 1900, Russia took control of all Persian customs, but it was on the Gulf which was under the control of England that limited them.

In 1907, the British recognized the Russian sphere of influence in the north and Russia recognized a British influence in the south.

Imperial ambitions had deepened the hostility between Great Britain and Russia and disputes over the Indian borderland added fuel to the quarrel they had long waged over the Ottoman empire (until the 1907 settlement). In addition, the struggle for African colonies had at the same time estranged England from France and it was at this time that these countries had their famous showdown at Fashoda in 1899 where the French backed down.

CHINA BEFORE WESTERN PENETRATION

In the Old China view, China was the world itself, the middle kingdom between the Upper and Nether regions. In reality, China was a land continually rocked by revolutions against the Manchus, the greatest of all upheavals being the Tai-Ping Rebellion of 1850.

This was the period when China's warlords first arose. They were men controlling armed forces but obeying no government. The Tai-Ping Rebellion was put down after fourteen years by means of European help. An outstanding figure in the action was Sir George Gordon (also known as the Chinese Gordon), who later died at Khartoum.

It is clear that China's social confusion, agrarianism, and nationalism all weakened the last years of the Manchu dynasty. All these forces antedate the impact of European imperialism.

According to most historians, Chinese relations with the West began with the Opium War in 1841 after which the English got most of the Chinese trade via selling Indian opium, the one product the English had which the Chinese desired. When the Chinese government attempted to regulate its own trade with the Europeans, Chinese interference was blasted away.

Byron Farwell, discussing the famous Opium War states that the emperor of China was kept completely isolated from the realities of the situation[3] much as Robert Payne was kept isolated from reality while he did research for his biography of Adolph Hitler in the New York Public Library. Farwell also shows that the English government paid its sailors money for each Chinese pirate they killed.[4]

While the Rebecca Riots took place in Wales (1839, 1842-49) London was in the midst of the Chartism issue (1838-48). Queen Victoria's "Little Wars" also included the 1843 war in Sind, which today is called Pakistan.

England and France forced the Chinese government to accept European diplomats as equals and enforced their point by looting the Summer Palace in Peking. The loot, when it was transferred to Europe, set a fashion for Chinese art, still prevalent today now that the United States and Mao Tse-tung's China are again friends.

The Treaty of Tientsin (1857) conferred certain rights on foreigners in China. The Treaty of Nanking in 1842 had given the English government rule over Hong Kong.

All along the coast of China treaty ports were established in which European settlements were governed by the laws of their own countries. The Chinese, provoked into war and defeated, naturally paid a war indemnity and agreed not to levy any customs above 5 percent in any Chinese ports. Customs inspectors in these ports were Europeans.

"Imagine what the United States would be like if foreign war-ships patrolled the Mississippi River as far as St. Louis; if for-eigners came and went throughout the country without being under its laws; if New York, New Orleans, and other cities con-tained foreign settlements outside their jurisdiction, but in which all banking and management were concentrated; if foreigners determined the tariff policies, collected the proceeds, and remitted much of the money to their own governments; if the western part of the city of Washington had been burned as the Summer Palace was; if Long Island and California were annexed to distant em-pires [Hong Kong and Indochina], and if all New England were coveted by two immediate neighbors [Manchuria] and if all national authorities were half in collusion with these foreigners and half victimized by them; and if large areas of the country were the prey of bandits, guerrillas, and revolutionary secret societies conspiring against the helpless government [and occa-sionally murdering some of the foreigners]. Now he can under-stand how observant Chinese felt at the end of the last century and why the word 'Imperialism' came to be held by so many of the world's peoples in abomination."[5]

Among the European nations that partitioned China, Russia was a strong contender for the title of Number 1. A part of China known historically as the Maritime Province (the area where Vladivostok now stands) was taken in 1960.

The French came to Vietnam in 1883, and the British arrived in Burma in 1886. The Japanese recognized "Korean Independ-ence" in 1876. Korea had had important political and cultural relations with China and paid tribute to her until the twentieth century when South Korea fell under the protection of the United States. The late Chung Yee Park would not comment about this.

JAPANESE IMPERIALISM

In 1895, the Japanese declared war on China. The Japanese, trained by the Germans, easily defeated the Chinese and the Peace Treaty of Shimonoseki was signed in 1895. In the treaty China ceded Korea, Formosa, and Liaotung Peninsula to Japan. That peninsula incidentally is a tongue of land extending from Manchuria to the sea. At its tip stood Port Arthur which was a great Russian naval base.

In 1891 the Russians began to build the Trans-Siberian Railroad. They felt that whether or not they themselves ever dominated Manchuria, they could not allow its domination by any other power.

About the same time it happened that Germany was looking for a chance to enter the Far Eastern area and France had formed an alliance with Russia whose good will it was eager to maintain. Pressure from France forced Japan to give up the Liaotung Peninsula, but the Japanese were permitted to keep Korea and Formosa.

THE EVILS OF WESTERN IMPERIALISM

China began modernizing madly after 1898, but what historians called "The Chinese Scramble" continued. The Germans leased the Kiaoshow Bay area in 1898. The Russians leased the Liaotung Peninsula. The French, being concerned with their "glory," took Kwangchow; and the British lion bared its claws and forced the Chinese to lease to them the Port of Wei-hai-wei. The English also confirmed their sphere of influence in the Yangtze valley.

The newly-unified Italian government demanded a share of the spoils and was refused. (They had a similar experience in Ethiopia.) The Italian army had a record of success second only to that of the Egyptian army.

The United States now stepped into the scene. According

to Palmer, the United States acted because they feared that all China might soon be parceled out into exclusive spheres. Historically this policy, known as the policy of the "Open Door," was not so much a matter of leaving China to the Chinese as it was of assuring that all outsiders should find China literally open.[6]

In 1899, the Chinese had reached the limit of their endurance and throughout the country a popular organization sprang up. It was called the Order of Literary, Patriotic, Harmonious Fists and it was foremost in an uprising called the Boxer Rebellion.

This rebellion was temporarily successful in besieging certain European governmental legations. Finally a relief expedition had to be sent to Peking. It was commanded by a German general since everybody knew that the Germans, following Prussian tradition, were the most efficient military people in the world. After this rebellion was put down by European forces, China paid an indemnity. (The United States got $24 million, but cancelled most of the money in 1924.)

In 1904 the Russo-Japanese War was provoked by Japan's surprise attack on Port Arthur which successfully destroyed most of the Russian fleet. It was the first time a fight had occurred between two industrialized powers. A Japanese excuse was that since 1895 Russian railroad rights through Manchuria had been disturbing them. In 1902, England and Japan signed a treaty of alliance.

During the Russo-Japanese War the battle of Mukden, in which 624,000 men were engaged, was the largest land battle up to that time. Russia's defeat spurred the Czarist government to call home its Baltic fleet. The Russian fleet was ambushed in Tshushima Strait and practically annihilated.

At this time pressure from the United States forced the combatants to agree to peace, which was solemnized at Portsmouth. As Palmer pointed out, the United States did not want either side to win too overwhelmingly.

Results

1. The first war brought general powers since 1870. It was

the first war fought under conditions of developed imperialism.

2. It was the first war between westernized powers to be caused by competition in the exploitation of backward countries. And if these two statements seem involved, consider how involved it will be when Russia, Japan, China, and England are all in different dimensions.

3. According to Palmer, the most significant fact of that war was that it was the first time that a colored people had defeated a white people in modern times.

Long-Range Results

1. One long-range result of the Russo-Japanese War was that the Russian government shifted its attention away from Asia and back to Europe. According to L.S. Stavrianov writing in the Berkshire series, Russian concentration in the Balkans between 1815-1914 provoked World War I.

2. A second result of that war was that even before the defeat of the Russian fleet, the Russian revolution of 1905 had broken out in Moscow. That revolution was merely one of God's preludes to the great Russian revolution of 1917 which led to communism.

3. Throughout Asia there were nationalistic revolutions. Persia had one in 1905. Turkey had one in 1908, and China had one in 1911.

The Japanese victory and the Russian defeat can be seen as mere steps in God's plan for human development. Other parts of this plan were World War I, the Russian revolutions, and the revolt in Asia which has temporarily been climaxed by American victory in Vietnam.

All three of these developments in God's plan ended world supremacy for the Europeans.

Appendix I

A CONTRAST BETWEEN THE
AMERICAN AND BRITISH VIEW OF GOD

This historian recently saw two delightful movies. One was *Tom Sawyer* and the other was *Mary Poppins*. In the former there is a delightful song called "If I Was God," in which Tom, a typical American boy, relates how he would make everybody wise.

The *Mary Poppins* film is a strong contrast with the *Tom Sawyer* movie. Throughout the film, which takes place in England, there is a strong emphasis on money. To this historian the contrast indicates clearly that William the Conqueror's win at Hastings in 1066 meant everything in England was his to give away.

God, however, has use for the English-speaking people. For that reason many great discoveries began in England. For example, in 1865 Isaac Singer invented the sewing machine.

The God this historian believes in is to be found in Exodus 15. There are many American Jews who doubt that this God could possibly be so cruel. Most American Jews, including my father, would prefer to believe in the God to be found in the book *The Joys of Yiddish* by Leo Rosten. In the immortal words of my mother, "So good."

In this historian's opinion, Americans are God's chosen people. As proof of this fact, it is suggested that the interested reader look at the *Conservationist Magazine* for October-November, 1972. On the cover of that issue there is a typical American church steeple.

Within its pages, however, the usual ridiculous articles are to be discovered. There is, for example, one article which claims

that New York's farmers are an endangered species. The article
also claims that traditions and customs of the people of upper
New York state are passing away, and furthermore, that the
values described in Oliver Goldsmith's poems are disappearing.
In this historian's opinion, this article is also garbage. Again,
books and articles are both out of date.

Another happy contrast between America and England is to
be found in the national game, observing baseball, where the
British take things immensely seriously. Only in America do the
young people of all races, creeds, colors, and religions mix and
blend. The New York Mets, for example, have a club for young-
sters called the Midget Mets. The Yankees celebrate Bat Day
where every youngster gets a little bat free.

Returning to the God I believe in, this historian recommends
Exodus 15, Numbers 17. The latter verse describes my death
far in advance. "When I die, as all men do . . ." Until that time,
however, this historian plans to continue writing book after
book.

As a further contrast between England and America, it might
be observed that a Jew in England is always a foreigner. As my
readers know, a Jew in America is simply a Jewish American.
God, in his majesty, has continually surprised me.

The British National game soccer is just as delightful. God
chose both the English and the Americans in the 1970s for a
world of New Dimensions.

On page ix in *The Diary of John Evelyn*[1] (1635-1706) there
is a discussion of two men, one good and one evil, which con-
cludes with pious words and the question as to why God lets the
evil man succeed while the good man fails. If this historian were
asked this question, he would answer "Karma" because no human
being can possibly know all of God's secrets.

In the same context, this historian has frequently stated that
England and America do not speak the same language. A clear
example of this fact is before me. It is a flyer from Fanwood
for the coming election. This is a Republican flyer. It argues
that "Fanwood needs Joan Geer and John Hawlet." This historian

has not yet seen the Democratic flyer. Therefore, I have not yet made up my mind whom I will vote for.

There is a clear contrast between American elections and English elections. It is my understanding that in England one votes either Conservative or Labor, depending on which party one's father favored. In the same way, this historian would be the last person in the world to criticize England's history because it is a historical fact that England gave us the Common Law.

England also had the first Industrial Revolution and much of the world was colonized by England. There was a happy period when most of the maps of the world were painted red, which represented the British Empire, but in the words of God and this historian, "Those days are gone forever."

ENGLAND: THE NATIONAL STATE
AND THE NATIONAL CHARACTER

The reason Parliament has had a much greater success in England than have similar bodies on the Continent lies in the fact that, in critical epochs, royalty there was strong enough to ensure internal peace, together with a measure of national unity, while the nobility, backed by the middle classes, was strong enough to prevent the king from becoming too powerful. But it was perhaps the salient point in the evolution of English characteristics that the upper class at least got the better of royalty through the support of large sections of other classes. God says splendid, splendid.

Although there are numerous books about the great European family of bankers, the Rothschilds, the fact that their activities inspired Adolph Hitler to destroy 5½ million Jews is usually ignored. All the precise dates in that sequence of events are to be found in the article on page 167 of *The Central European History Journal* of June 1973.

In Willson's book, Prime Minister Pitt is discussed on page 490.[2] Pelham and Pitt were very important historical figures in the Seven Years War (1756-63).

Throughout Shakespeare's plays, there are code words that show me why some Europeans hate each other. For example, in *Henry V*, Englishmen are urged to sink their swords into the French for Henry, England, and St. George. The Duke of Gloucester is another important figure. The Americans and the English obviously have a great deal in common. On the one hand the English love birds and other pets and it is an English naturalist who is shown in the *Monitor* of January 9 saving the White Rhinoceros from extinction in Africa. But God continues to work in front of everybody.

For example, a long article in the January 11, 1974, *Christian Science Monitor* shows that a new treaty between the United States and Panama is being negotiated. Few people remember it was an American president, Teddy Roosevelt, who created Panama.

The English are always shown to be remaking the world. God used them as he is using the Americans today. In 1577 Sir Francis Drake sailed around the world, and that shows the English bearing the message of Christianity to the uncivilized inhabitants of the other continents.

There is a great similarity between the English and the Americans, to be seen, for instance, in the way the two peoples began their respective civil wars. As Bruce Catton shows on page 187,[3] the American Civil War, which began shortly after Fort Sumter was fired on, really had its inception among men who did not want to kill other men. The English Civil War began in much the same way in the seventeenth century.

In the book by Thorne, Lockner and Smith the famous War of Jenkin's Ear of 1740 is discussed.[4] This historian, who knows that the Egyptian Third Army was trapped in the Sinai Desert by the Jews, firmly believes in the God of Abraham, Isaac and Jacob who is at work everywhere.

It is interesting to learn that the Hanoverian dynasty which is still ruling in England was established in 1742.

There is far more detail about England's world trade from page 402.[4] There is a brief discussion of the method by which the English gained control of India and an equally brief one of the way the English gained control of large parts of China. It is interesting to learn that our state of Georgia was established by the English in 1733. It is this historian's sincere hope that the marriage of Princess Ann and Mark Phillips, will be as happy as his own marriage.

I believe that the English-speaking people run the world. I well recall thoughts I had before my marriage. The longer I live, the more convinced I am that as far as the United States is concerned, running the world is our most important job. Thus, in 1961 the Russians were forced to withdraw their missiles from Cuba. In 1973, they were forced to back out on their promise of troops for the Arabs when President Nixon mobilized the Armed Forces of the United States.

Most recently, I was immensely gratified that Soyuz 13 had been forced to land early because of a malfunction. I hated the Russians during World War II even while we were fighting the same enemies.

One of my heroes is Abraham Lincoln. I strongly believe that both sides in our stupid Civil War were fighting on God's side and the good guys won.

I am in the midst of Lacey Baldwin Smith's book *This Realm of England* and it strikes me as spiritually significant that the Wars of the Roses began in 1453. Those English wars involved Marguerite of Anjou and King Henry VI of England. These two, representing the Lancastrians, were fighting Richard, the Duke of York. Those wars had the Roses name because the Lancastrians used red roses as their symbol, while the Yorkists used white roses. Those silly wars were fought with countless scrimmages which used up the cowards of England. For example, the Battle of Towten saw the Lancastrians terribly defeated. As Smith brings out, the weather during that battle was a blowing snow storm.[5]

Later, during those wars, Edward IV (1461-83) married Elizabeth Woodville (in 1464), ruining the hopes of Warwick, known historically as the King Maker. Edward IV diplomatically allied England with the Duchy of Burgundy, which naturally involved France, then ruled by King Louis XI. During the course of these events, English princes were murdered in the Tower of London.

HISTORICAL RELATIVITY, OR WHY
THE UNITED STATES OF AMERICA
IS THE ONLY COUNTRY IN THE WORLD
TO REALLY KNOW WHAT IT MEANS
WHEN IT SAYS ANYTHING

In a German book about English history, the author, Hopfel, criticizes English historians for being critical of German imperialism but ignoring the evils of British imperialism.[6] An article by Godfried Goerer, a sociologist, points out that Englishmen cannot understand other Englishmen if they move thirty miles away from home.

This lack of understanding is prevalent throughout the entire world. Only the United States of America means what the President says it means. As President Nixon was quoted as saying when criticized about his policies on Vietnam, "It isn't what we say, but what we do that counts."*

As I have attempted to point here, words are relative in their meanings. It was quite appropriate that Albert Einstein should have given the earth-shaking theory of relativity to the world since Einstein was a Jew; and in God's world, the Jews are God's chosen people.

My comments are in answer to an article by Jeffrey Hart, entitled "Guernica," in the *National Review* of January 5, 1973, in which he attempts to prove from his vast reading (two books are cited) that the German bombing of Guernica during the Spanish War in 1938 never happened.

Simultaneously an article by Phillip Abbot Luce, entitled "Whatever Happened to New York?" (*New Guard,* May 1972) admitted in more than one place that he did not know quite what he was saying, but that he was sure some of his readers would. In particular, I refer to his comments regarding the

---

*New Guard, May 1972.

Student Democratic Society having been killed by the Popular Labor Party. In conclusion, referring to President Nixon's statement, only the words of the President of the United States have any meaning in this insane world we live in. (See Kissinger's words in the United States State Department release—December 16, 1972.)

Appendix II

God was working throughout the reign of Elizabeth I (1558-1603) when He caused Peter Wentworth to defend freedom of speech in Parliament. It is directly from such court cases in England that the lies printed in *The New York Times* have spread. One cannot criticize any of the means of communication found in America, although one can have very strong feelings about some of the people who speak on American television. For example, the German author Hermann Boll was recently on *Speaking Freely* with the moderator Edwin Newman. Boll, who lived through Nazi Germany and was wounded four times, explained candidly that he has always opposed the ideas of Nazism. I myself had been sure that he was one of the millions of German soldiers who meekly and tacitly obeyed all the orders of the Führer. Boll stated that he believed the Constitution of the Weimar Republic had been a great one, but he neglected to mention that it was the faults within that Constitution that enabled Adolph Hitler to take power in Germany legally.

It is ironic to me that West Germany is exactly as old as the modern state of Israel. God is a very funny conceptualization Who works wonders in plain sight of all those who refuse to see what He is doing. I look forward to reading Boll's novel *The Clown,* because I am sure I will find many German code words that will go far in explaining to me more about the Nazi period. Boll explained that Hitler's strength had been in the countryside and in particular around Cologne, Hamburg, etc., the old cities of the *Hansa* in Germany. Boll concluded his statement by arguing that the Russian Army had no place in Germany. Unfortunately, few Russian politicians were listening to him, and the Russian army continues to occupy East Germany for good rational political reasons.

51

Religion has always been of great importance in the world. Thus, Hermann Boll was right when he said that Pope John, who died in 1964, had accomplished great things for the Catholic Church. Boll maintains that the Church today needs a new dimension and definition. I personally believe that it should be abolished.

Notes

I. ENGLISH HISTORY IN FIVE DIMENSIONS

1. Winston Churchill, *The Birth of Britain* in *History of the English-Speaking Peoples* (New York: Bantam, 1971).
2. David C. Douglas, *William the Conqueror: The Norman Impact Upon England* (Berkeley: University of California Press, 1964), p. 7.
3. Lacey Baldwin Smith, *This Realm of England: 1399 to 1688,* Second Edition (Lexington, Massachusetts: D. C. Heath and Co., 1971).
4. *Ibid.* p. 62.
5. Melvin C. Wren, *The Course of Russian History* (New York: The Macmillan Company, 1968), p. 205.
6. Smith, *op. cit.,* p. 65.
7. *Ibid.,* p. 76.
8. *Ibid.,* p. 81.
9. *Ibid.,* p. 83.
10. *Ibid.,* p. 83.
11. *Ibid.,* p. 85.
12. *Ibid.,* p. 113.
13. *Ibid.,* p. 115.
14. *Ibid.,* p. 154.
15. William E. Lunt, *History of England,* Third Edition (New York: Harper & Row, 1945), p. 337.
16. Smith, *op. cit.,* p. 181.
17. *Ibid.,* p. 181.
18. *Ibid.,* p. 182.

19. *Ibid.*, p. 185.
20. *Ibid.*, p. 182.
21. *Ibid.*, p. 184.
22. *Ibid.*, p. 186.
23. *Ibid.*, pp. 186-87.
24. *Ibid.*, p. 187.
25. *Ibid.*, p. 188.
26. *Ibid.*, p. 189.
27. *Ibid.*, p. 190.
28. *Ibid.*, p. 190.
29. *Ibid.*, p. 190.
30. *Ibid.*, p. 190.
31. *Ibid.*, pp. 191-92.
32. *Ibid.*, p. 193.
33. *Ibid.*, p. 200.
34. *Ibid.*, p. 201.
35. *Ibid.*, p. 207.
36. *Ibid.*, p. 207.
37. *Ibid.*, p. 229.
38. *Ibid.*, p. 231.

II. ENGLAND IN THE NINETEENTH AND TWENTIETH CENTURIES

1. Ralph G. Marlin, *Jennie,* Vol. I, *The Romantic Years* (Englewood Cliffs, New Jersey: Prentice-Hall, 1969.)
2. Lacey Baldwin Smith, *This Realm of England: 1399 to 1688,* Second Edition (Lexington, Massachusetts: D. C. Heath and Co., Ltd., 1971).
3. Keith Feiling, *A History of England* (London: Macmillan and Co., Ltd., 1963).
4. Edmund Curtis, *A History of Ireland* (New York: Barnes

& Noble, Inc. [University Paperbacks], 1961), pp. 376-88.

5. Robert R. Palmer and Joel Colton, *History of the Modern World,* Fourth Edition (New York: Alfred A. Knopf, 1971).

6. John B. Harrison and Richard E. Sullivan, *Short History of Western Civilization,* Third Edition (New York: Alfred A. Knopf, 1971), p. 517.

7. William E. Lunt, *History of England,* Third Edition (New York: Harper and Brothers, 1945), p. 690.

8. George D. Cole and Raymond Postgate, *British Common People* (New York: Barnes & Noble [University Paperbacks], 1961), p. 36.

9. Lunt, *op cit.,* p. 794.

10. George Dangerfield, *The Strange Death of Liberal England* (New York: G. P. Putnam, 1961), p. 144.

11. Ralph G. Martin, *Jennie,* Vol. II, *The Dramatic Years* (Englewood Cliffs, New Jersey: Prentice-Hall, 1971), p. 31.

III. COLONIALISM AND IMPERIALISM

1. Frank N. Henderson and William Henderson, *Communist China, 1949-1969: A Twenty Year Assessment* (New York: New York University Press, 1970), p. 241.

2. Kavalam M. Panniker, *Asia and Western Dominance* (New York: The Macmillan Company, 1969).

3. Byron Farwell, *Queen Victoria's Little Wars* (New York: Harper & Row, 1972), p. 20.

4. Farwell, *Ibid.,* p. 21.

5. Robert R. Palmer and Joel Colton, *History of the Modern World,* Fourth Edition (New York: Alfred A. Knopf, 1971), p. 665.

6. Palmer, *op. cit.,* p. 655.

APPENDIX I

1. John Evelyn, *Diary of John Evelyn* (Akron, Ohio: Walter Dunn, 1901), Vol. I, p. ix.

2. D. H. Willson, *History of England* (New York: Holt, Rinehart and Winston, 1967), p. 490.

3. Bruce Catton, *Coming Fury*, Vol. I, *Centennial History of the Civil War* (New York: Doubleday and Co., 1961), p. 187.

4. J. Thorne, R. Lockner and D. Smith, *A History of England* (New York: Thomas Y. Crowell Company, 1961).

5. Lacey Baldwin Smith, *This Realm of England: 1399 to 1688,* Second Edition (Lexington, Massachusetts: D. C. Heath and Co., 1971).

6. Hopfil, *Geschichte Englands und des Commonwealth* (Frankfurt am Main: Scheffler, 1965).